The Life and Opinions of Tristram Shandy, Gentleman. ... The Fifth Edition. of 9

THE

LIFE and OPINIONS

OF

TRISTRAM SHANDY, Gent.

Si quid urbaniufcule lufam a nobis, per Mufas et Charitatem
et omnium poetarum Numina, Oro te, ne me male capias.

VOL. IX.

CHAP. I.

I CALL all the powers of time and chance, which,
feverally check us in our careers in this world, to
bear me witnefs, that I could never yet get fairly to my
uncle Toby's amours, till this very moment, that my
mother's *curiofity*, as fhe ftated the affair,——or a different impulfe in her, as my father would have it——wifhed her to take a peep at them through the key-hole.

" Call it, my dear, by its right name, quoth my father, and look thro' the key-hole as long as you will."

Nothing but the fermentation of that little fubacid
humour, which I have often fpoken of, in my father's
habit, could have vented fuch an infinuation——he was
however frank and generous in his nature, and at all
times open to conviction; fo that he had fcarce got
to the laft word of this ungracious retort, when his
confcience fmote him.

My mother was then conjugally fwinging with her
left arm twifted under his right, in fuch wife, that the
infide of her hand refted upon the back of his——fhe
raifed her fingers, and let them fall——it could fcarce be
called a tap; or if it was a tap——'twould have puzzled
a cafuift to fay, whether 'twas a tap of remonftrance,

or

or a tap of confession : my father, who was all senfi-
bilities fiom head to foot, clafs'd it right—Confcience
redoubled her blow—he turn'd his face fuddenly the
other way, and my mother fuppofing his body was
about to turn with it in order to move homewards, by
a crofs movement of her right leg, keeping her left as
its centre, brought herfelf fo far in front, that as he
turn'd his head, he met her eye——Confufion again !
he faw a thoufand reafons to wipe out the reproach,
and as many to reproach himfelf——a thin, blue, chill,
pellucid chryftal with all its humours fo at reft, the leaft
mote or fpeck of defire might have been feen at the
bottom of it, had it exifted—it did not—and how I
happen to be fo lewd myfelf, particularly a little before the vernal and autumnal equinoxes——Heaven
above knows—My mother—Madam—was fo at no
time, either by nature, by inftitution, or example.

A temperate current of blood ran orderly through
her veins in all months of the year, and in all critical
moments both of the day and night alike; nor did
fhe fuperinduce the leaft heat into her humours from
the manual effervefcencies of devotional tracts, which
having little or no meaning in them, nature is oft-times
obliged to find one——And as for my father's example ! 'twas fo far from being either aiding or abetting
thereunto, that 'twas the whole bufinefs of his life
to keep all fancies of that kind out of her head—Nature had done her part, to have fpared him this trouble, and what was not a little inconfiftent, my father
knew it——And here am I fitting, this 12th day of
Auguft, 1766, in a purple jerkin and yellow pair of
flippers, without either wig or cap on, a moft tragi-
comical completion of his prediction, " That I fhould
neither think nor act like any other man's child, upon that very account "

The miftake of my father, was in attacking my mother's motive, inftead of the act itfelf, for certainly
key holes were made for other purpofes ; and confi-
dering the act, as an act which interfered with a true
propofition, and denied a key hole to be what it was
—it became a violation of nature, and was fo far, you
fee, criminal.

It

It is for this reason, an' pleafe your reverences, That key-holes are the occasions of more sin and wickednefs, than all other holes in this world put together.

—Which leads me to my uncle Toby's amours.

C H A P. II.

THOUGH the corporal had been as good as his word in putting my uncle Toby's great ramallie-wig into pipes, yet the time was too fhort to produce any gieat effects from it: it had lain many years fqueezed up in the corner of his old campaign trunk; and as bad forms aie not fo eafy to be got the better of, and the ufe of candle-ends not fo well underftood, it was not fo pliable a bufinefs as one would have wifhed. The corporal with cheaiy eye and both, arms extended, had fallen back perpendiculai from it a fcore times, to infpire it, if poffible, with a better air—Had SPLEEN given a look at it, 'twould have coft her ladyfhip a fmile——It curled every where but where the corporal would have it; and where a buckle or two, in his opinion, would have done it honour, he could as foon have raifed the dead.

Such it was—or rather fuch would it have feemed upon any other brow; but the fweet look of goodnefs which fat upon my uncle Toby's, affimilated every thing around it fo fovereignly to itfelf, and Nature had moreover wrote GENTLEMAN with fo fair a hand in every line of his countenance, that even his tarnifh'd gold-laced hat and huge cockade of flimfy taffeta became him; and though not worth a button in themfelves, yet the moment my uncle Toby put them on, they became ferious objects, and altogether feemed to have been picked up by the hand of Science to fet him off to advantage.

Nothing in this world could have co-operated more powerfully towards this, than my uncle Toby's blue and gold——*had not Quantity in fome meafuie been neceffary to Grace* · in a period of fifteen or fixteen years fince they had been made, by a total inactivity in my uncle Toby's life, foi he feldom went furthei than

the

the bowling-green—his blue and gold had become fo
miferably too ftrait for him, that it was with the ut-
moft difficulty the corporal was able to get him into
them : the taking them up at the fleeves, was of no
advantage.————They were laced however down
the back, and at the feams of the fides, &c. in the
mode of King William's reign ; and to fhorten all de-
fcription, they fhone fo bright againft the fun that
morning, and had fo metallic and doughty an air with
them, that had my uncle Toby thought of attacking
in armour, nothing could have fo well impofed upon
his imagination.

As for the thin fcarlet breeches they had been un-
ripp'd by the taylor between the legs, and left at *fixes
and fevers*————

————Yes, Madam,—but let us govern our fancies.
It is enough they were held impracticable the night
before ; and as there was no alternative in my uncle
Toby's wardrobe, he fallied forth in the red plufh.

The corporal had array'd himfelf in poor Le Fevre's
regimental coat ; and with his hair tuck'd up under
his Montero-cap, which he had furbifh'd up for the
occafion, march'd three paces diftant from his mafter :
a whiff of military pride had puffed out his fhirt at
the wrift ; and upon that, in a black leather thong
clipp'd into a taffel beyond the knot, hung the corporal's ftick—My uncle Toby carried his cane like a
pike ——

—It looks well at leaft, quoth my father to himfelf.

CHAP. III

MY uncle Toby turn'd his head more than once
behind him, to fee how he was fupported by
the corporal ; and the corporal, as oft as he did it,
gave a flight flourifh with his ftick—but not vapour-
ingly ; and with the fweeteft accent of moft refpectful
encouragement, bid his honour " never fear."

Nor my uncle Toby did fear ; and grievoufly too :
he knew not (as my father had reproached him) fo
much as the right end of a woman from the wrong,
and

and therefore was never altogether at his eafe near any
one of them—unlefs in forrow or diftrefs : then infi
nite was his pity ; nor would the moft courteou
knight of romance have gone further, at leaft upon on
leg, to have wiped away a tear from a woman's eye ;
and yet excepting once that he was beguiled into it by
Mrs Wadman, he had never looked ftedfaftly into
one ; and would often tell my father in the fimplicity
of his heart, that it was almoft (if not all out) as bad
as talking bawdy————
————And fuppofe it is ? my father would fay.

C H A P. IV.

SHE cannot, quoth my uncle Toby, halting, when
they had marched up to within twenty paces of
Mrs Wadman's door————fhe cannot, corporal, take it
amifs————

—She will take it, an' pleafe your honour, faid the
corporal, juft as the Jew's widow at Lifbon took it of
my brother Tom.————

—And how was that ? quoth my uncle Toby, facing quite about to the corporal.

Your honour, replied the corporal, knows of Tom's
misfortunes ; but this affair has nothing to do with
them any further than this, That if Tom had not married the widow—or had it pleafed God after their marriage, that they had but put pork into their faufages,
the honeft foul had never been taken out of his warm
bed, and dragg'd to the inquifition————'Tis a curfed
place—added the corporal, fhaking his head—when
once a poor creature is in, he is in, an' pleafe your honour, for ever.

'Tis very true, faid my uncle Toby, looking gravely at Mrs Wadman's houfe, as he fpoke.

Nothing, continued the corporal, can be fo fad as
confinement for life—or fo fweet, an' pleafe your honour, as liberty.

Nothing, Trim—faid my uncle Toby, mufing—
Whilft

Whilſt a man is free—cried the corporal, giving a flouriſh with his ſtick thus——

A thouſand of my father's moſt ſubtle ſyllogiſms could not have ſaid more for celibacy.

My uncle Toby looked earneſtly towards his cottage and his bowling-green.

The corporal had unwarily conjured up the ſpirit of calculation with his wand; and he had nothing to do, but to conjure him down again with his ſtory, and in this form of exorciſm, moſt unecclefiaſtically did the corporal do it.

C H A P. V.

AS Tom's place, an' pleaſe your honour, was eaſy —and the weather warm——it put him upon thinking ſeriouſly of ſettling himſelf in the world; and as it fell out about that time, that a Jew, who kept a
ſauſage

faufage-fhop in the fame ftreet, had the ill luck to die of a ftranguiy, and leave his widow in poffeffion of a roufing trade—Tom thought (as every body in Lifbon was doing the beft he could devife for himfelf) there could be no harm in offeiing her his fervice to carry it on : fo, without any introduction to the widow, except that of buying a pound of faufages at her fhop—Tom fet out—counting the matter thus within himfelf, as he walked along; that, let the worft come of it that could, he fhould at leaft get a pound of faufages for their worth—but, if things went well, he fhould be fet up; inafmuch as he fhould get not only a pound of faufages—but a wife—and a faufage-fhop, an' pleafe your honour, into the bargain.

Every fervant in the family, from high to low, wifhed Tom fuccefs; and I can fancy, an' pleafe your honour, I fee him this moment with his white dimity waiftcoat and breeches, and hat a little o'one fide, paffing jollily along the ftreet, fwinging his ftick, with a fmile and a chearful word for every body he met: But, alas! Tom! thou fmileft no moie, cried the corporal, looking on one fide of him upon the ground, as if he apoftrophized him in his dungeon.

Poor fellow! faid my uncle Toby, feelingly.

He was an honeft, light-hearted lad, an' pleafe your honour, as ever blood warm'd—

——Then he refembled thee, Trim, faid my uncle Toby, rapidly.

The corporal blufhed down to his fingers ends—a tear of fentimental bafhfulnefs—anothei of gratitude to my uncle Toby—and a tear of forrow for his brother's misfoitunes, ftarted into his eye, and ran fweetly down his cheek together; my uncle Toby's kindled, as one lamp does at anothei ; and taking hold of the breaft of Trim's coat (which had been that of Le Fevre's) as if to eafe his lame leg, but in reality to gratify a finer feeling—he ftood filent for a minute and a half; at the end of which he took his hand away, and the corporal making a bow, went on with his ftoiy of his biothei and the Jew's widow.

CHAP.

C H A P. VI.

WHEN Tom, an' pleafe your honour, got to the fhop, there was no body in it, but a poor negro girl, with a bunch of white feathers flightly tied to the end of a long cane, flapping away flies——not killing them—'Tis a pretty picture! faid my uncle Toby—fhe had fuffered perfecution, Trim, and had learned mercy——

—She was good, an' pleafe your honour, from nature as well as from hardfhips; and there are circumftances in the ftory of that poor friendlefs flut, that would melt a heart of ftone, faid Trim, and fome difmal winter's evening, when your honour is in the humour, they fhall be told you with the reft of Tom's ftory, for it makes a part of it——

Then do not forget, Trim, faid my uncle Toby.

A negro has a foul? an' pleafe your honour, faid the corporal (doubtingly.)

I am not much verfed, corporal, quoth my uncle Toby, in things of that kind; but I fuppofe, God would not leave him without one, any more than thee or me——

—It would be putting one fadly over the head of another, quoth the corporal.

It would be fo; faid my uncle Toby. Why then, an' pleafe your honour, is a black wench to be ufed worfe than a white one?

I can give no reafon, faid my uncle Toby——

—Only, cried the corporal, fhaking his head, becaufe fhe has no one to ftand up for her——

—'Tis that very thing, Trim, quoth my uncle Toby,—which recommends her to protection—and her brethren with her; 'tis the fortune of war which has put the whip into her hands *now*—where it may be hereafter, heaven knows!—but be it where it will, the brave, Trim! will not ufe it unkindly.

—God forbid, faid the corporal.

Amen, refponded my uncle Toby, laying his hand upon his heart.

The

The corporal returned to his ſtory, and went on—
but with an embarraſſment in doing it, which here
and there a reader, in this world, will not be able
to comprehend; for by the many ſudden tranſi-
tions all along, from one kind and cordial paſſion to
another, in getting thus far on his way, he had loſt
the ſportable key of his voice which gave ſenſe
and ſpirit to his tale: he attempted twice to re-
ſume it, but could not pleaſe himſelf; ſo giving a
ſtout hem! to rally back the retreating ſpirits, and
aiding Nature at the ſame time with his left arm a-
kimbo on one ſide, and with his right a little extended, ſupporting her on the other, the corporal got as
near the note as he could; and in that attitude, continued his ſtory.

C H A P. VII.

AS Tom, an' pleaſe your honour, had no buſineſs
at that time with the Mooriſh girl, he paſſed
on into the room beyond, to talk to the Jew's widow
about love————and his pound of ſauſages; and
being, as I had told your honour, an open, cheary-
hearted lad, with his character wrote in his looks and
carriage, he took a chair, and without much apology,
but with great civility at the ſame time, placed it cloſe
to her at the table, and ſat down.

There is nothing ſo awkward, as courting a woman, an' pleaſe your honour, whilſt ſhe is making
ſauſages————So Tom began a diſcourſe upon
them; firſt gravely,————as, "How they were made
————with what meats, herbs and ſpices"————Then
a little gayly————as, "With what ſkins————and if
they never burſt————Whether the largeſt were not
the beſt"————and ſo on————taking care only, as he
went along, to ſeaſon what he had to ſay upon ſauſages, rather under, than over;—that he might have
room to act in————

It was owing to the neglect of that very precaution,
ſaid my uncle Toby, laying his hand upon Trim's ſhoul-
der, that Count de la Motte loſt the battle of Wynen-
dale: he preſſed too ſpeedily into the wood; which if
he

he had not done, Lifle had not fallen into our hands, nor Ghent and Bruges, which both followed her example; it was fo late in the year, continued my uncle Toby, and fo terrible a feafon came on, that if things had not fallen out as they did, our troops muft have perifhed in the open field ——

——Why therefore may not battles, an' pleafe your honour, as well as marriages, be made in heaven?—— My uncle Toby mufed.——

Religion inclined him to fay one thing, and his high idea of military fkill tempted him to fay another, fo not being able to frame a reply exactly to his mind— my uncle Toby faid nothing at all; and the corporal finifhed his ftory.

As Tom perceived, an' pleafe your honour, that he gained ground, and that all he had faid upon the fubject of faufages was kindly taken, he went on to help her a little in making them—Firft, by taking hold of the ring of the faufage, whilft fhe ftroaked the forced meat down with her hand—then by cutting the ftrings into proper lengths, and holding them in his hand, whilft fhe took them out, one by one—then by putting them acrofs her mouth, that fhe might take them out as fhe wanted them—and fo on from little to more, till at laft he adventured to tie the faufage himfelf, whilft fhe held the fnout.

——Now, a widow, an' pleafe your honour, always chufes a fecond hufband as unlike the firft as fhe can: fo the affair was more than half fettled in her mind before Tom mentioned it.

She made a feint, however, of defending heifelf by fnatching up a faufage : Tom inftantly laid hold of another——

But feeing Tom's had more griftle in it——

She figned the capitulation——and Tom fealed it; and there was an end of the matter.

C H A P. VIII.

ALL womankind, continued Trim, (commenting upon his ftory) from the higheft to the loweft, an' pleafe your honour, love jokes ; the difficulty is to

know

know how they chufe to have them cut ; and there is
no knowing that, but by trying, as we do with our ar-
tillery in the field, by raifing or letting down their
breaches, till we hit the mark.———

———I like the comparifon, faid my uncle Toby,
better than the thing itfelf.———

———Becaufe your honour, quoth the corporal, loves
glory more than pleafure.

——I hope, Trim, anfwered my uncle Toby, I love
mankind more than either; and as the knowledge of
arms tends fo apparently to the good and quiet of the
world—and particularly that branch of it which we have
practifed together in our bowling-green, has no object
but to fhorten the ftrides of AMBITION, and entrench
the lives and fortunes of the *few*, from the plunderings
of the *many*—whenever that drum beats in our ears, I
truft, corporal, we fhall neither of us want fo much
humanity and fellow-feeling as to face about and march.

In pronouncing this, my uncle Toby faced about,
and marched firmly, as at the head of his company—
and the faithful corporal, fhouldering his ftick, and
ftriking his hand upon his coat-fkirt, as he took his
firft ftep—marched clofe behind him down the avenue.

——Now what can their two noddles be about ? cried my father to my mother———by all that's ftrange,
they are befieging Mrs Wadman in form, and are
marching round her houfe to mark out the lines of
circumvallation.

I dare fay, quoth my mother—But ftop, dear Sir,
—for what my mother dared to fay upon the occafion—and what my father did fay upon it—with her
replies and his rejoinders, fhall be read, perufed, para-
phrafed, commented, and difcanted upon—or, to fay
it all in a word, fhall be thumb'd over by Pofterity in
a chapter apart—I fay, by Pofterity—and care not,
if I repeat the word again—for what has this book
done more than the Legation of Mofes, or the Tale
of a Tub, that it may not fwim down the gutter of
Time along with them ?

I will not argue the matter : Time waftes too faft :
every letter I trace tells me with what rapidity Life follows my pen; the days and hours of it, more precious,

my

my dear Jenny ! than the rubies about thy neck, are
flying over our heads, like light clouds of a windy day,
never to return more—every thing preffes on—whilft
thou art twifting that lock,—fee ! it grows grey; and
every time I kifs thy hand, to bid adieu, and every ab-
fence which follows it, are preludes to that eternal fe-
paration which we are fhortly to make.——
—Heaven have mercy upon us both !

C H A P. IX.

NOW, for what the world thinks of that ejacula-
tion—I would not give a groat.

C H A P. X.

MY mother had gone with her left arm twifted
in my father's right, till they had got to the
fatal angle of the old garden wall where Dr Slop was
overthrown by Obadiah on the coach-horfe : as this
was directly oppofite to the front of Mrs Wadman's
houfe, when my father came to it, he gave a look a-
crofs ; and feeing my uncle Toby and the corporal
within ten paces of the door, he turned about——
" Let us juft ftop a moment, quoth my father, and
fee with what ceremonies my brother Toby and his
man Trim make their firft entry——it will not
detain us, added my father, a fingle minute."——
No matter, if it be ten minutes, quoth my mother.
——It will not detain us half a one, faid my
father.
The corporal was juft then fetting in with the ftory
of his brother Tom and the Jew's widow. the ftory
went on—and on—it had epifodes in it—it came back,
and went on—and on again ; there was no end of it—
the reader found it very long——
—G— help my father ! he pifh'd fifty times at e-
very new attitude, and gave the corporal's ftick, with
all its flourifhings and danglings, to as many devils as
chofe to accept of them.
When iffues of events like thefe my father is waiting
for, are hanging in the fcales of fate, the mind has the
advantage

advantage of changing the principle of expectation three times, without which it would not have power to fee it out.

Cuiiofity governs the *firft moment;* and the fecond moment is all œconomy, to juftify the expence of the firft—and for the thiid, fourth, fifth, and fixth moments, and fo on to the day of judgment—'tis a point of Honour.

I need not be told, that the ethic writers have affigned this all to Patience, but that Virtue, methinks, has extent of dominion fufficient of her own, and enough to do in it, without invading the few difmantled caftles which Honour has left him upon the earth.

My father ftood it out as well as he could with thefe thiee auxiliaries to the end of Trim's ftory, and from thence to the end of my uncle Toby's panegyric upon arms, in the chapter following it, when feeing, that inftead of marching up to Mrs Wadman's door, they both faced about and maiched down the avenue, diametrically oppofite to his expectation—he broke out at once with that little fubacid fournefs of humour which, in certain fituations, diftinguifhed his character from that of all other men.

CHAP. XI.

———" NOW what can their two noddles be about ?" cried my father—&c.———

I dare fay, faid my mother, they are making fortifications——

—Not on Mrs Wadman's premifes! cried my father, ftepping back——

I fuppofe not, quoth my mother.

I wifh, faid my father, raifing his voice, the whole fcience of fortification at the devil, with all its trumpery of faps, mines, blinds, gabions, fauffe-brays and cuvettes——

—They are foolifh things—faid my mother.

Now fhe had a way, which, by the bye, I would this moment give away my purple jeikin, and my yellow flippers into the bargain, if fome of your reverences would imitate————and that was, never to refuse her assent and consent to any proposition my father laid before her, merely because she did not understand it, or had no ideas to the principal word or term of art, upon which the tenet or proposition rolled. She contented herself with doing all that her godfathers and godmothers promised for her————but no more; and so would go on using a hard word twenty years together—and replying to it too, if it was a verb, in all its moods and tenses, without giving herself any trouble to enquire about it.

This was an eternal source of misery to my father, and broke the neck, at the first setting out, of more good dialogues between them, than could have done the most petulant contradiction—the few which survived were the better for the *cuvettes.*————

—" They are foolish things," said my mother.

—Particularly the *cuvettes,* replied my father.

'Twas enough—he tasted the sweet of triumph———and went on .

————Not that they are, properly speaking, Mrs Wadman's premises, said my father, partly correcting himself—because she is but tenant for life————

————That makes a great difference—said my mother————

—In a fool's head, replied my father————

Unless she should happen to have a child—said my mother————

—But she must persuade my brother Toby first to get her one————

—To be sure, Mr Shandy, quoth my mother.

—Though if it comes to persuasion—said my father—Lord have mercy upon them.

Amen: said my mother, *piano.*

Amen: cried my father, *fortissime.*

Amen: said my mother again————but with such a sighing cadence of personal pity at the end of it, as discomfited every fibre about my father————he instantly took out his almanack. but before he could untie it, Yorick's congregation coming out of church, became a full answer to one half of his business with it—and my mother telling him it was a sacrament-day—left

him

him as little in doubt, as to the other part—He put
his almanack into his pocket.

The firſt lord of the treaſury, thinking of *ways and
means*, could not have returned home, with a more
embarraſſed look.

C H A P. XII.

UPON looking back from the end of the laſt chapter, and ſurveying the texture of what has been
wrote, it is neceſſary, that upon this page and the
five following, a good quantity of heterogeneous matter be inſerted, to keep up that juſt balance betwixt
wiſdom and folly, without which a book would not
hold together a ſingle year nor is it a poor creeping
digreſſion (which, but for the name of, 'a man might
continue as well going on in the king's high-way)
which will do the buſineſs—no, if it is to be a digreſſion, it muſt be a good friſky one, and upon a friſky
ſubject too, where neither the horſe or his rider are to
be caught, but by rebound

The only difficulty, is raiſing powers ſuitable to the
nature of the ſervice Fancy is capricious——Wit
muſt not be ſearched for—and Pleasantry (good-
natured ſlut as ſhe is) will not come in at a call, was
an empire to be laid at her feet.

—The beſt way for a man, is to ſay his prayers—

Only if it puts him in mind of his infirmities and
defects, as well ghoſtly as bodily —for that purpoſe,
he will find himſelf rather worſe, after he has ſaid
them, than before—for other purpoſes, better.

For my own part, there is not a way, either moral or
mechanical under heaven, that I could think of, which
I have not taken with myſelf in this caſe; ſometimes
by addreſſing myſelf directly to the ſoul herſelf, and
arguing the point over and over again with her, upon
the extent of her own faculties——

—I never could make them an inch the wider——

Then, by changing my ſyſtem, and trying what
could be made of it upon the body, by temperance,
ſoberneſs and chaſtity. Theſe are good, quoth I, in
themſelves—they are good, abſolutely ,——they are

Q 2   good,

good, relatively ;—they are good for health——they are good for happineſs in this world—they are good for happineſs in the next——

In ſhort, they were good for every thing but the thing wanted; and there they were good for nothing, but to leave the ſoul juſt as heaven made it : as for the theological virtues of faith and hope, they give it courage ; but then that ſnivelling virtue of Meekneſs (as my father would always call it) takes it quite a-way again, ſo you are exactly where you ſtarted.

Now, in all common and ordinary caſes, there is no-thing which I have found to anſwer ſo well as this——

—Certainly, if there is any dependence upon Logic, and that I am not blinded by ſelf-love, there muſt be ſomething of true genius about me, merely upon this ſymptom of it, that I do not know what envy is : for never do I hit upon any invention or device which tendeth to the furtherance of good writing, but I in-ſtantly make it public, willing that all mankind ſhould write as well as myſelf.

—Which they certainly will, when they think as little.

C H H P. XIII.

NOw in ordinary caſes, that is, when I am only ſtupid, and the thoughts riſe heavily and paſs gummous through my pen——

Or that I am got, I know not how, into a cold un-metaphorical vein of infamous writing, and cannot take a plumb-lift out of it *for my ſoul ;* ſo muſt be o-bliged to go on writing like a Dutch commentator to the end of the chapter, unleſs ſomething be done——

—I never ſtand conferring with pen and ink one moment; for if a pinch of ſnuff, or a ſtride or two acroſs the room, will not do the buſineſs for me—I take a razor at once ; and having tried the edge of it upon the palm of my hand, without further ceremony, except that of firſt lathering my beard, I ſhave it off ; taking care only if I do leave a hair, that it be not a gray one: this done, I change my ſhirt—put on a bet-ter coat——ſend for my laſt wig—put my topaz ring

upon

upon my finger; and, in a word, drefs myfelf from one end to the other of me, after my beft fafhion.

Now the devil in hell muft be in it, if this does not do; for confider, Sir, as every man choofes to be prefent at the fhaving of his own beard (though there is no rule without an exception) and unvoidably fits over againft himfelf the whole time it is doing, in cafe he has a hand in it——the Situation, like all others, has notions of her own to put into the brain——

—I maintain it, the conceits of a rough-bearded man, are feven years more terfe and juvenile for one fingle operation; and if they did not run a rifk of being quite fhaved away, might be carried up by continual fhavings, to the higheft pitch of fublimity—— How Homer could write with fo long a beard, I don't know——and as it makes againft my hypothefis, I as little care——But let us return to the toilet.

Ludovicus Sorbonensis, makes this entirely an affair of the body (ἐξωτερικὴ πραξις) as he calls it— but he is deceived: the foul and body are joint-fharers in every thing they get: A man cannot drefs, but his ideas get clothed at the fame time; and if he drefſes like a gentleman, every one of them ftands prefented to his imagination, genteelized along with him——fo that he has nothing to do, but take his pen, and write like himfelf.

For this caufe, when your honours and reverences would know whether I write clean and fit to be read, you will be able to judge full as well by looking into my Laundrefs's bill, as my book. there was one fingle month in which I can make it appear, that I dirtied one and thirty fhirts with clean writing; and after all, was more abufed, curfed, criticifed, and confounded, and had more myftic heads fhaken at me, for what I had wrote in that one month, than in all the other months of that year put together.

—But then honours and reverences had not feen my *bills.*

CHAP.

CHAP. XIV.

AS I never had any intention of beginning the
Digreſſion, I am making all this preparation
for, till I come to the 15th chapter——I have this
chapter to put to whatever uſe I think proper——I
have twenty this moment ready for it——I could write
my chapter of Button-ho'es in it——

Or my chapter of Piſnes, which ſhould follow
them——

Or my chapter of Knots, in caſe their reverences
have done with them—they might lead me into miſ-
chief: the ſafeſt way is to follow the tract of the
learned, and raiſe objections againſt what I have been
writing, tho' I declare beforehand, I know no more
than my heels how to anſwer them.

And firſt, it may be ſaid, there is a pelting kind of
therſitical ſatire, as black as the very ink 'tis wrote
with—(and, by the bye, whoever ſays ſo, is indebted
to the muſter-maſter general of the Grecian army,
for ſuffering the name of ſo ugly and foul-mouth'd a
man as Therſites to continue upon his roll—for it has
furniſhed him with an epithet)—in theſe productions
he will urge, all the perſonal waſhings and ſcrubbings
upon earth do a ſinking genius no ſort of good—but
juſt the contrary, inaſmuch as the dirtier the fellow
is, the better generally he ſucceeds in it.

To this, I have no other anſwer—at leaſt ready—
but that the archbiſhop of Benevento wrote his naſty
Romance of the Galatea, as all the world knows, in
a purple coat, waiſtcoat, and purple pair of breeches,
and that the penance ſet him, of writing a commenta-
ry upon the book of the Revelations, as ſevere as it
was looked upon by one part of the world, was far
from being deemed ſo by the other, upon the ſingle
account of that inveſtment.

Another objection to all this remedy, is its want
of univerſality, foraſmuch as the ſhaving part of it,
upon which ſo much ſtreſs is laid, by an unalterable
law of nature, each deſerts one half of the ſpecies entirely

f,om

from its ufe : all I can fay is, that female writers, whether of England, or of France, muft e'en go with- out it————

As for the Spanifh ladies————I am in no fort of diftrefs.————

C H A P. XV.

THE fifteenth chapter is come at laft ; and brings nothing with it but a fad fignatme of " How our pleafures flip from under us in this world '"

For in talking of my digreffion————I declare be- fore heaven I have made it ! What a ftrange creature is mortal man ! faid fhe.

'Tis very true, faid I—but 'twere better to get all thefe things out of our heads, and return to my uncle Toby.

C H A P. XVI.

WHEN my uncle Toby and the corporal had marched down to the bottom of the avenue, they recollected their bufinefs lay the other way ; fo they faced about, and marched up ftraight to Mrs Wadman's door.

I warrant your honour ; faid the corporal, touch- ing his Montero-cap with his hand, as he paffed him in order to give a knock at the door—My uncle To- by, contrary to his invariable way of treating his faith- ful fervant, faid nothing good or bad: the truth was, he had not altogether marfhalled his ideas ; he wifhed for another conference, and as the corporal was mount ing up the three fteps before the door———he hemm'd twice————a portion of my uncle Toby's moft modeft fpirits fled, at each expulfion, towards the corporal ; he ftood with the rapper of the door fufpended for a full minute in his hand, he fcarce knew why. Bridget ftood perdue within, with her finger and her thumb upon the latch, benumbed with expectation ; and Mrs Wadman, with an eye ready to be deflowered again, fat breathlefs behind the window-curtain of her bed- chamber, watching their approach.

Trim !

Trim! faid my uncle Toby—but as he articulated the word, the minute expired, and Trim let fall the rapper.

My uncle Toby, perceiving that all hopes of a conference were knock'd on the head by it——whiftled Lillabullero.

C H A P. XVII.

AS Mrs Bridget's finger and thumb were upon the latch, the corporal did not knock as oft as perchance your honour's taylor———I might have taken my example fomething nearer home ; for I owe mine fome five and twenty pounds at leaft, and wonder at the man's patience———

——But this is nothing at all to the world : only 'tis a curfed thing to be in debt; and there feems to be a fatality in the exchequers of fome poor princes, particularly thofe of our houfe, which no œconomy can bind down in irons . for my own part, I am perfuaded there is not any one prince, prelate, pope, or potentate, great or fmall upon earth, more defirous in his heart of keeping ftraight with the world than I am— or who takes more likely means for it. I never give above half a guinea—or walk with boots—or cheapen tooth-picks—or lay out a fhilling upon a band-box the year round ; and for the fix months I am in the country, I am upon fo fmall a fcale, that with all the good temper in the world, I outdo Roufleau, a bar length—for I keep neither man, or boy, or horfe, or cow, or dog, or cat, or any thing that can eat or drink, except a thin poor piece of a veftal (to keep my fire in) and who has generally as bad an appetite as myfelf—but if you think this makes a philofopher of me—I would not, my good people ! give a rufh for your judgments.

True philofophy———But there is no treating the fubject whilft my uncle is whiftling Lillabullero.

———Let us go into the houfe.

C H A P. XVIII.

C H A P. XIX.

C H A P. XX.

———— ❋ ❋ ❋ ❋ ❋ ❋ ❋
❋ ❋ ❋ ❋ ❋ ❋ ❋ ❋ ❋
❋ ❋ ❋ ❋.
❋ ❋ ❋ ❋ ❋ ❋ ❋ ❋ ❋
❋ ❋ ❋ ❋ ❋ ❋ ❋ ❋ ❋
❋ ❋ ❋ ❋ ❋ ❋ ❋.————

—You fhall fee the very place, Madam; faid my uncle Toby.

Mrs Wadman blufh'd—look'd towards the door—turn'd pale—blufh'd flightly again————recovered her natural colour—————blufhed worfe than ever; which, for the fake of the unlearned reader, I tranflate thus.————

" *L—d! I cannot look at it————*
What would the world fay if I look'd at it ?
I fhould drop down if I look'd at————
I wifh I could look at it————
There can be no fin in looking at it.
————" *I will look at it* "

Whilft all this was running through Mrs Wadman's imagination, my uncle Toby had rifen from the fopha, and got to the other fide of the parlour-door, to give Trim an order about it in the paffage————

❋ ❋ ❋ ❋ ❋ ❋ ❋ ❋ ❋

❋ ❋————I believe it is in the garret, faid my uncle Toby——I faw it there, an' pleafe your honour, this morning, anfwered Trim——Then Pr'ythee, ftep directly for it, Trim, faid my uncle Toby, and bring it into the parlour.

The corporal did not approve of the orders, but moft chearfully obeyed them. The firft was not an act of his will——the fecond was; fo he put on his Montero-cap, and went as faft as his lame knee would let him. My uncle Toby returned into the parlour, and fat himfelf down again upon the fopha.

—You fhall lay your finger upon the place—faid my uncle Toby—I will not touch it, however, quoth Mrs Wadman to herfelf.

This

This requires a fecond tranflation:—it fhews what little knowledge is got by mere words—we muft go up to the firft fprings.

Now, in order to clear up the mift which hangs upon thefe three pages, I muft endeavour to be as clear as poffible myfelf

Rub your hands thrice acrofs your foreheads—blow your nofes—cleanfe your emunctories——fneeze, my good people '—God blefs you——

Now give me all the help you can.

C H A P. XXI.

AS there are fifty different ends (counting all ends in—as well civil as religious) for which a woman takes a hufband, fhe firft fets about and carefully weighs, then feparates and diftinguifhes in her mind, which of all that number of ends is hers. then by difcourfe, enquiry, argumentation and inference, fhe inveftigates and finds out whether fhe has got hold of the right one——and if fhe has——then, by pulling it gently this way and that way, fhe further forms a judgment, whether it will not break in the drawing.

The imagery under which Slawkenbergius impreffes this upon his reader's fancy, in the beginning of his third Decad, is fo ludicrous, that the honour I bear the fex, will not fuffer me to quote it—otherwife 'tis not deftitute of humour.

"She firft, faith Slawkenbergius, ftops the afs, and holding his halter in her left hand (left he fhould get away) fhe thrufts her right hand into the very bottom of his pannier to fearch for it—For what !——you'll not know the fooner, quoth Slawkenbergius, for interrupting me——

" I have nothing, good lady, but empty bottles ;" fays the afs.

" I am loaded with tripes," fays the fecond.

—And thou art little better, quoth fhe to the third; for nothing is there in thy panniers but trunk-hofe and pantoufles—and fo to the fourth and fifth, going on one by one through the whole ftring, till coming to the

the afs which carries it, fhe turns the pannier upfide
down, looks at it—confiders it—famples it—meafures
it—ftretches it—wets it—dries it——then takes her
teeth both to the warp and weft of it——

—Of what? for the love of Chrift!

I am determined, anfwered Slawkenbergius, that
all the powers upon earth fhall never wring that fecret from my breaft.

C H A P. XXII.

WE live in a world befet on all fides with myfte-
ries and riddles————and fo 'tis no matter————elfe it feems ftrange, that Nature, who
makes every thing fo well to anfwer its deftination,
and feldom or never errs, unlefs for paftime, in giving
fuch forms and aptitudes to whatever paffes through
her hands, that whether fhe defigns for the plough,
the caravan, the cart—or whatever other creature fhe
models, be it but an afs's foal, you are fure to have the
thing you wanted; and yet at the fame time fhould
fo eternally bungle it as fhe does, in making fo fimple
a thing as a married man.

Whether it is in the choice of the clay—or that it
is frequently fpoiled in the baking; by an excefs of
which a hufband may turn out too crufty (you know)
on one hand——or not enough fo, through defect of
heat, on the other—or whether this great Artificer is
not fo attentive to the little Platonic exigencies *of that
part* of the fpecies, for whofe ufe fhe is fabricating *this*
—or that her Ladyfhip fometimes fcarce knows what
fort of a hufband will do—I know not: we will difcourfe about it after fupper.

It is enough, that neither the obfervation itfelf, or
the reafoning upon it, are at all to the purpofe—but
rather againft it; fince, with regard to my uncle Toby's
fitnefs for the marriage ftate, nothing was ever better:
fhe had formed him of the beft and kindheft clay—had
temper'd it with her own milk, and breathed into it the
fweeteft fpirit—fhe had made him all gentle, generous
and humane——fhe had fill'd his heart with truft and
confidence,

confidence, and difpofed every paffage which led to
it, for the communication of the tendereft offices——
fhe had moreover confidered the other caufes for which
matrimony was ordained————

And accordingly   *   *   *   *
*   *   *   *   *   *   *
*   *   *   *   *   *   *
*   *.

The DONATION was not defeated by my uncle Toby's wound.

Now this laft article was fomewhat apocryphal;
and the devil, who is the great difturber of our faiths
in this world, had raifed fcruples in Mrs Wadman's
brain about it, and like a true devil as he was, had
done his own work at the fame time, by turning my
uncle Toby's virtue thereupon into nothing but *empty
bottles, tripes, trunk-hofe,* and *pantoufles.*

C H A P. XXIII.

MRS Bridget had pawn'd all the little ftock of
honour a poor chambermaid was worth in the
world, that fhe would get to the bottom of the affair
in ten days; and it was built upon one of the moft
conceffible *poftulatum* in nature: namely, that whilft
my uncle Toby was making love to her miftrefs, the
corporal could find nothing better to do, than make
love to her——" *And I'll let him as much as he will,*"
faid Bridget, " *to get it out of him.*"

Friendfhip has two garments; an outer, and an
under one. Bridget was ferving her miftrefs's inter-
refts in the one——and doing the thing which moft
pleafed herfelf in the other, fo had as many ftakes
depending upon my uncle Toby's wound, as the devil himfelf——Mrs Wadman had but one——and as it
poffibly might be her laft (without difcouraging Mrs
Bridget, or difcrediting her talents) was determined to
play her cards herfelf.

She wanted not encouragement. a child might have
look'd into his hand—there was fuch a plainnefs and
fimplicity in his playing out what trumps he had—

witk

with fuch an unmiftrufting ignorance of the *ten-ace*—
and fo naked and defencelefs did he fit upon the fame
fopha with widow Wadman, that a generous heart
would have wept to have won the game of him.

Let us drop the metaphor.

C H A P. XXIV.

— A ND the ftory too—if you pleafe: for though
I have all along been haftening towards this
part of it, with fo much earneft defire, as well knowing it to be the choiceft morfel of what I had to offer
to the world, yet now that I am got to it, any one is
welcome to take my pen, and go on with the ftory
for me that will—I fee the difficulties of the defcrip-
tions I am going to give——and feel my want of
powers.

It is one comfort at leaft to me, that I loft fome
fourfcore ounces of blood this week, in a moft uncriti-
cal fever, which attacked me at the beginning of this
chapter; fo that I have ftill fome hopes remaining, it
may be more in the ferous or globular parts of the
blood, than in the fubtle *aura* of the brain——be it
which it will—an Invocation can do no hurt—and I
leave the affair entirely to the *invoked*, to infpire or to
inject me according as he fees good.

THE INVOCATION.

G ENTLE Spirit of fweeteft humour, who erft
didft fit upon the eafy pen of my beloved CER-
VANTES; Thou who glided'ft daily through his lat-
tice, and turned'ft the twilight of his prifon into noon-
day brightnefs by thy prefence——tinged'ft his little
urn of water with heaven-fent Nectar, and all the
time he wrote of Sancho and his mafter, didft caft thy
myftic mantle o'er his wither'd * ftump, and wide extended it to all the evils of his life————

———TURN

---

* He loft his hand at the battle of Lepanto.

—Turn in hither, I befeech thee!—behold thefe breeches!——they are all I have in the world—that piteous rent was given them at Lyons.——

My fhirts! fee what a deadly fchifm has happened amongft 'em—for the laps are in Lombardy, and the reft of 'em here—I never had but fix, and a cunning gipfy of a laundrefs at Milan cut me off the *fore-laps* of five—To do her juftice, fhe did it with fome confideration—for I was returning *out* of Italy.

And yet, notwithftanding all this, and a piftol tin-der-box which was, moreover, filch'd from me at Sienna, and twice that I paid five Pauls for two hard eggs, once at Raddicoffini, and a fecond time at Ca-pua—I do not think a journey through France and I-taly, provided a man keeps his temper all the way, fo bad a thing as fome people would make you believe : there muft be *ups* and *downs*, or how the duce fhould we get into vallies where Nature fpreads fo many tables of entertainment —'Tis nonfenfe to imagine they will lend you their voitures to be fhaken to pieces for no-thing, and unlefs you pay twelve fous for greafing your wheels, how fhould the poor peafant get butter to his bread?——We really expect too much—— and for the livre or two above par for your fuppers and bed——at the moft, they are but one fhilling and nine-pence halfpenny——who would embroil their philofophy for it? for heaven's and for your own fake, pay it——pay it with both hands open, ra-ther than leave *Difappointment* fitting drooping up-on the eye of your fair Hoftefs and her Damfels in the gate-way, at your departure—and befides, my dear Sir, you get a fifterly kifs of each of 'em worth a pound—at leaft I did——

——For my uncle Toby's amours running all the way in my head, they had the fame effect upon me as if they had been my own—I was in the moft perfect ftate of bounty and good will, and felt the kindlieft harmony vibrating within me, with every ofcillation of the chaife alike ; fo that whether roads were rough or fmooth, it made no difference, every thing I faw, or had to do with, touch'd upon fome fecret fpring ei-ther of fentiment or rapture.

—They

——They were the sweeteft notes I ever heard; and I inftantly let down the fore-glafs to hear them more diftinctly——'Tis Maria; faid the poftilion, obferving I was liftening—Poor Maria, continued he, (leaning his body on one fide to let me fee her, for he was in a line betwixt us) is fitting upon a bank, playing her vefpers upon her pipe, with her little goat befide her.

The young fellow utter'd this with an accent and a look fo perfectly in tune to a feeling heart, that I inftantly made a vow, I would give him a four and twenty fous piece, when I got to *Moulins*——

——And who is *poor Maria?* faid I.

The love and pity of all the villages around us; faid the poftilion—it is but three years ago, that the fun did not fhine upon fo fair, fo quick-witted and amiable a maid; and better fate did Maria deferve, than to have her Banns forbid, by the intrigues of the curate of the parifh who publifhed them——

He was going on, when Maria, who had made a fhort paufe, put the pipe to her mouth and began the air again——they were the fame notes,——yet were ten times fweeter: It is the evening fervice to the Virgin, faid the young man—but who has taught her to play it——or how fhe came by her pipe, no one knows; we think that Heaven has affifted her in both; for ever fince fhe has been unfettled in her mind, it feems her only confolation——fhe has never once had the pipe out of her hand, but plays that *fervice* upon it almoft night and day.

The poftilion delivered this with fo much difcretion and natural eloquence, that I could not help decyphering fomething in his face above his condition, and fhould have fifted out his hiftory, had not poor Maria's taken fuch full poffeffion of me

We had got up by this time almoft to the bank where Maria was fitting · fhe was in a thin white jacket, with her hair, all but two treffes, drawn up into a filk net, with a few olive leaves twifted a little fantaftically on one fide—fhe was beautiful; and if ever I felt the full force of an honeft heart ache, it was the moment I faw her——

—God help her! poor damsel: above a hundred masses, said the postilion, have been said in the several parish churches and convents around, for her——but without effect; we have still hopes, as she is sensible for short intervals, that the Virgin at last will restore her to herself, but her parents, who know her best, are hopeless upon that score, and think her senses are lost for ever.

As the postilion spoke this, Maria made a cadence so melancholy, so tender and querulous, that I sprung out of the chaise to help her, and found myself sitting betwixt her and her goat, before I relapsed from my enthusiasm.

Maria looked wistfully for some time at me, and then at her goat—and then at me——and then at her goat again, and so on alternately——

—Well, Maria, said I softly—what resemblance do you find?

I do intreat the candid reader to believe me, that it was from the humblest conviction of what a *Beast* man is,—that I ask'd the question, and that I would not have let fallen an unseasonable pleasantry in the venerable presence of Misery, to be entitled to all the wit that ever Rabelais scatter'd—and yet I own my heart smote me, and that I so smarted at the very idea of it, that I swore I would set up for Wisdom, and utter grave sentences the rest of my days—and never—never attempt again to commit mirth with man, woman, or child, the longest day I had to live.

As for writing nonsense to them—I believe, there was a reserve—but that I leave to the world.

Adieu, Maria!—adieu, poor hapless damsel!—— some time, but not *now*, I may hear thy sorrows from thy own lips—but I was deceived, for that moment she took her pipe, and told me such a tale of woe with it, that I rose up, and with broken and irregular steps, walk'd softly to my chaise.

—What an excellent inn at Moulins!

CHAP.

C H A P. XXV.

WHEN we have got to the end of this chapter (but not before) we muſt all turn back to the two blank chapters, on the account of which my honour has lain bleeding this half hour——I ſtop it, by pulling off one of my yellow ſlippers, and throwing it with all my violence to the oppoſite ſide of my room, with a declaration at the heel of it——

——That whatever reſemblance it may bear to half the chapters which are written in the world, or, for aught I know, may be now writing in it—that it was as caſual as the foam of Zeuxis his horſe : beſides, I look upon a chapter which has *only nothing in it*, with reſpect, and conſidering what worſe things there are in the world—That it is no way a proper ſubject for ſatire——

Why then was it left ſo? And here, without ſtaying for my reply, ſhall I be called as many blockheads, numſculs, doddypoles, dunderheads, ninnyhammers, gooſecaps, joltheads, nincompoops, and ſh t a-beds—— and other unſavoury appellations, as ever the cake-bakers of Lerne, caſt in the teeth of King Garagantua's ſhepherds————And I'll let them do it, as Bridget ſaid, as much as they pleaſe; for how was it poſſible they ſhould foreſee the neceſſity I was under of writing the 25th chapter of my book, before the 18th, &c.

——So I don't take it amiſs——All I wiſh is, that it may be a leſſon to the world, *" to let people tell their ſtories their own way."*

The Eighteenth Chapter.

AS Mrs Bridget open'd the door before the corporal had well given the rap, the interval betwixt that and my uncle Toby's introduction into the parlour, was ſo ſhort, that Mrs Wadman had but juſt time to get from behind the curtain—lay a Bible upon the table, and advance a ſtep or two towards the door to receive him.

My

My uncle Toby faluted Mrs Wadman, after the manner in which women were faluted by men in the year of our Lord God one thoufand feven hundred and thirteen———————then facing about, he marched up abreaft with her to the fopha, and in three plain words————though not before he was fat down———nor after he was fat down—but as he was fitting down, told her, " *he was in love*"——————fo that my uncle Toby ftrained himfelf more in the declaration than he needed.

Mrs Wadman naturally looked down upon a flit fhe had been darning up in her apron, in expectation every moment, that my uncle Toby would go on; but having no talents for amplification, and Love more-over of all others being a fubject of which he was the leaft a mafter—when he had told Mrs Wadman once that he loved her, he let it alone, and left the matter to work after its own way.

My father was always in raptures with this fyftem of my uncle Toby's, as he falfely called it, and would often fay, that could his brother Toby to his proceffe have added but a pipe of tobacco————he had where-withal to have found his way, if there was faith in a Spanifh proverb, towards the hearts of half the wo-men upon the globe.

My uncle Toby never underftood what my father meant; nor will I prefume to extract more from it, than a condemnation of an error which the bulk of the world lie under————but the French, every one of 'em to a man, who believe in it, almoft as much as the REAL PRESENCE, " *That talking of love, is making it* "

————I would as foon fet about making a black-pudding by the fame receipt.

Let us go on : Mrs Wadman fat in expectation my uncle Toby would do fo, to almoft the firft pulfation of that minute, wherein filence, on one fide or the o-ther, generally becomes indecent; fo edging herfelf a little more towards him, and raifing up her eyes, fub-blufhing, as fhe did it—fhe took up the gauntlet—or the difcourfe (if you like it better) and communed with my uncle Toby, thus :

The

The cares and difquietudes of the marriage ftate, quoth Mrs Wadman, are very great. I fuppofe fo—faid my uncle Toby. and therefore, when a perfon, continued Mrs Wadman, is fo much at his eafe as you are——fo happy, Captain Shandy, in yourfelf, your friends, and your amufements—I wonder, what reafons can incline you to the ftate.——

——They are written, quoth my uncle Toby, in the Common Prayer Book

Thus far my uncle Toby went on warily, and kept within his depth, leaving Mrs Wadman to fail upon the gulph as fhe pleafed.

—As for children——faid Mrs Wadman——though a principal end perhaps of the inftitution, and the natural wifh, I fuppofe, of every parent——yet do not we all find, they are certain forrows, and very uncertain comforts? and what is there, dear Sir, to pay one for the heart-aches—what compenfation for the many tender and difquieting apprehenfions of a fuffering and defencelefs mother who brings them into life? I declare, faid my uncle Toby, fmit with pity, I know of none; unlefs it be the pleafure which it has pleafed God——

——A fiddleftick! quoth fhe.

Chapter the Nineteenth.

NOW there are fuch an infinitude of notes, tunes, cants, chants, airs, looks, and accents with which the word *fiddleftick* may be pronounced in all fuch caufes as this, every one of 'em impreffing a fenfe and meaning as different from the other, as *dirt* from *cleanlinefs*—That Cafuifts (for it is an affair of confcience on that fcore) reckon up no lefs than fourteen thoufand, in which you may do either right or wrong.

Mrs Wadman hit upon the *fiddleftick*, which fummoned up all my uncle Toby's modeft blood into his cheeks—fo feeling within himfelf that he had fomehow or other got beyond his depth, he ftopt fhort, and without entering further either into the pains or pleafures of matrimony, he laid his hand upon his heart, and made

R 3

an

an offer to take them as they were, and fhare them along with her.

When my uncle Toby had faid this, he did not care to fay it again, fo cafting his eye upon the Bible which Mrs Wadman had laid upon the table, he took it up ; and popping, dear foul' upon a paffage in it, of all others the moft interefting to him—which was the fiege of Jericho—he fet himfelf to read it over— leaving his propofal of marriage, as he had done his declaration of love, to work with her after its own way. Now, it wrought neither as an aftringent or a loofener; nor like opium, or bark, or mercury, or buckthorn, or any one drug which Nature had beftowed upon the world—in fhort, it work'd not at all in her, and the caufe of that was, that there was fomething working there before—Babbler that I am ! I have anticipated what it was a dozen times; but there is fire ftill in the fubject—allons.

C H A P. XXVI.

IT is natural for a perfect ftranger, who is going from London to Edinburgh, to enquire, before he fets out, how many miles to York; which is about the half way—nor does any body wonder, if he goes on and afks about the Corporation, &c. - -

It was juft as natural for Mrs Wadman, whofe firft hufband was all his time afflicted with a fciatica, to wifh to know how far from the hip to the groin; and how far fhe was likely to fuffer more or lefs in her feel-ings, in the one cafe than in the other.

She had accordingly read Drake's anatomy, from one end to the other. She had peeped into Whatton upon the brain, and borrowed * Graaf upon the bones and mufcles ; but could make nothing of it.

She had reafon'd likewife from her own powers— laid down theorems—drawn confequences, and come to no conclufion.

To

---

* There muft be a miftake in Mr Shandy, for Graaf wrote upon the pancreatic juice, and the parts of generation

To clear up all, she had twice asked Dr Slop, " if poor Captain Shandy was ever likely to recover of his wound?"——

——He is recovered, Dr Slop would say.

What! quite?

——Quite, Madam——

But what do you mean by a recovery? Mrs Wadman would say.

Dr Slop was the worst man alive at definitions; and so Mrs Wadman could get no knowledge: in short, there was no way to extract it, but from my uncle Toby himself.

There is an accent of humanity in an inquiry of this kind, which lulls Suspicion to rest——and I am half persuaded the serpent got pretty near it, in his discourse with Eve , for the propensity in the sex to be deceived could not be so great, that she should have boldness to hold chat with the devil without it—— But there is an accent of humanity—how shall I describe it?—'tis an accent which covers the part with a garment, and gives the inquirer a right to be as particular with it as your body-surgeon.

" —Was it without remission?——

" —Was it more tolerable in bed?

" —Could he lie on both sides alike with it?

" —Was he able to mount a horse?

" —Was motion bad for it?" *et cætera*, were so tenderly spoke to, and so directed towards my uncle Toby's heart, that every item of them sunk ten times deeper into it than the evils themselves—but when Mrs Wadman went round about by Namur to get at my uncle Toby's groin; and engaged him to attack the point of the advanced counterscarp, and *pêle mêle* with the Dutch to take the counter guard of St Roch sword in hand—and then with tender notes playing upon his ear, led him all bleeding by the hand out of the trench, wiping her eye, as he was carried to his tent—Heaven ! Earth ! Sea !—all was lifted up—the springs of nature rose above their levels—an angel of mercy sat beside him on the sopha—his heart glow'd with fire——and had he been worth a thousand, he had lost every heart of them to Mrs Wadman.

——And

—And whereabouts, dear Sir, quoth Mrs Wadman, a little categorically, did you receive this sad blow?—In asking this question, Mrs Wadman gave a slight glance towards the waistband of my uncle Toby's red plush breeches, expecting naturally, as the shortest reply to it, that my uncle Toby would lay his forefinger upon the place—It fell out otherwise—for my uncle Toby having got his wound before the gate of St Nicolas, in one of the traverses of the trench, opposite to the salient angle of the demi-bastion of St Roch; he could at any time stick a pin upon the identical spot of ground where he was standing when the stone struck him: this struck instantly upon my uncle Toby's sensorium—and with it, struck his large map of the town and citadel of Namur and its environs, which he had purchased and pasted down upon a board by the corporal's aid, during his long illness—it had lain with other military lumber in the garret ever since, and accordingly the corporal was detached into the garret to fetch it.

My uncle Toby measured off thirty toises, with Mrs Wadman's scissars, from the returning angle before the gate of St Nicolas; and with such a virgin modesty laid her finger upon the place, that the goddess of Decency, if then in being—if not 'twas her shade—shook her head, and with a finger wavering across her eyes—forbid her to explain the mistake.

Unhappy Mrs Wadman!

—For nothing can make this chapter go off with spirit but an apostrophe to thee—but my heart tells me that, in such a crisis, an apostrophe is but an insult in disguise, and ere I would offer one to a woman in distress—let the chapter go to the devil, provided a-ry damn'd critic *in keeping* will be but at the trouble to take it with him.

C H A P. XXVII.

MY uncle Toby's map is carried down into the kitchen.

C H A P.

C H A P. XXVIII.

—— AND here is the Maes———and this is the Sambre, faid the corporal, pointing with his right hand extended a little towards the map, and his left upon Mrs Bridget's fhoulder———but not the fhoulder next him———and this, faid he, is the town of Namur———and this the citadel———and there lay the French—and here lay his honour and myfelf—and in this curfed trench, Mrs Bridget, quoth the corporal, taking her by the hand, did he receive the wound which crufh'd him fo miferably *here*—In pronouncing which, he flightly prefs'd the back of her hand towards the part he felt for—and let it fall.

We thought, Mr Trim, it had been more in the middle—faid Mrs Bridget———

That would have undone us for ever—faid the corporal.

——And left my poor miftrefs undone too—faid Bridget.

The corporal made no reply to the repartee, but by giving Mrs Bridget a kifs.

Come—come —faid Bridget—holding the palm of her left hand parallel to the plane of the horizon, and fliding the fingers of the other over it, in a way which could not have been done, had there been the leaft wart or protuberance———'Tis is every fyllable of it falfe, cried the corporal, before fhe had half finifhed the fentence———

—I know it to be fact, faid Bridget, from credible witneffes

——Upon my honour, faid the corporal, laying his hand upon his heart, and blufhing as he fpoke with honeft refentment—'tis a ftory, Mrs Bridget, as falfe as hell———Not, faid Bridget, interrupting him, that either I or my miftrefs care a halfpenny about it, whether 'tis fo or no—only that when one is married, one would choofe to have fuch a thing by one at leaft———

It was fomewhat unfortunate for Mrs Bridget, that fhe had begun the attack with her manual exercife, for

the

the corporal inftantly   *   *   *   *
*   *   *   *   *   *   *
*   *   *   *   *   *   *
*   *   *.

C H A P. XXIX.

IT was like the momentary conteft in the moift eye-
lids of an April morning, "Whether Bridget
fhould laugh or cry."

She fnatch'd up a rolling-pin—'twas ten to one fhe
had laugh'd———

She laid it down—fhe cried; and had one fingle
tear of 'em but tafted of bitternefs, full forrowful would
the corpo-al's heart have been that he had ufed the
argument; but the corporal underftood the fex, *a quart
major to a terce* at leaft, better than my uncle Toby,
and accordingly he affailed Mrs Bridget after this
manner.

I know, Mrs Bridget, faid the corporal, giving her
a moft refpectful kifs, that thou art good and modeft
by nature, and art withal fo generous a girl in thyfelf,
that, if I know thee rightly, thou wouldft not wound
an infect, much lefs the honour of fo gallant and wor-
thy a foul as my mafter, waft thou fure to be made a
countefs of——but thou haft been fet on, and deluded,
dear Bridget, as is often a woman's cafe, " to pleafe
others more than themfelves———"

Bridget's eyes poured down at the fenfations the
corporal excited———

—Tell me—tell me then, my dear Bridget, continued the corporal, taking hold of her hand, which hung
down dead by her fide—and giving a fecond kifs—
whofe fufpicion has mifled thee?

Bridget fobb'd a fob or two—then opened her eyes
———the corporal wiped 'em with the bottom of her
apron—fhe then open'd her heart and told him all.

C H A P. XXX.

MY uncle Toby and the corporal had gone on fe-
parately with their operations the greateft part
cf

of the campaign, and as effectually cut off from all communication of what either the one or the other had been doing, as if they had been separated from each other by the Maes or the Sambre.

My uncle Toby, on his side, had presented himself every afternoon in his red and silver, and blue and gold alternately, and suftained an infinity of attacks in them without knowing them to be attacks——and so had nothing to communicate——

The corporal, on his side, in taking Bridget, by it had gained confiderable advantages—and confequently had much to communicate—but what were the advantages——as well as what was the manner by which he had feized them, required fo nice an hiftorian that the corporal durft not venture upon it; and as fenfible as he was of glory, would rather have been contented to have gone bare-headed, and without laurels for ever, than torture his mafter's modefty for a fingle moment——

Beft of honeft and gallant fervants!——But I have apoftrophiz'd thee, Trim! once before—and could I apotheofize thee alfo (that is to fay) with good company——I would do it *without ceremony* in the very next page.

CHAP. XXXI.

NOW my uncle Toby had one evening laid down his pipe upon the table, and was counting over to himfelf, upon his finger ends, (beginning at his thumb) all Mrs Wadman's perfections, one by one; and happening two or three times together, either by omitting fome, or counting others twice over, to puzzle himfelf fadly before he could get beyond his middle finger——Pi'ythee Trim! faid he, taking up his pipe again,—bring me a pen and ink. Trim brought paper alfo.

Take a full fheet—Trim! faid my uncle Toby, making a fign with his pipe at the fame time to take a chair and fit down clofe by him at the table The corporal obeyed—placed the paper directly before him —took a pen and dipp'd it in the ink.

——She

—She has a thoufand virtues, Trim' faid my uncle
Toby——

Am I to fet them down, an' pleafe your honour?
quoth the corporal.

—But they muft be taken in their ranks, replied
my uncle Toby; for of them all, Trim, that which wins
me moft, and which is a fecurity for all the reft, is
the compaffionate turn and fingular humanity of her
character—I proteft, added my uncle Toby, looking
up, as he protefted it, towards the top of the cieling
—That was I her brother, Trim, a thoufand fold, fhe
could not make more conftant or more tender inquiries
after my fufferings—though now no more.

The corporal made no reply to my uncle Toby's
proteftation, but by a fhort cough—he dipp'd the pen
a fecond time into the ink-horn, and my uncle Toby,
pointing with the end of his pipe as clofe to the top
of the fheet, at the left hand corner of it, as he could
get it———the corporal wrote down the word HU-
MANITY - - - - thus.

Pr'ythee, corporal, faid my uncle Toby, as foon as
Trim had done it—how often does Mrs Bridget in-
quire after the wound on the cap of thy knee, which
thou receiv'd'ft at the battle of Landen?

She never, an' pleafe your honour, inquires after it
at all.

That, corporal, faid my uncle Toby, with all the
triumph the goodnefs of his nature would permit—
that fhews the difference in the character of the miftrefs and maid——Had the fortune of war allotted the
fame mifchance to me, Mrs Wadman would have inquired into every circumftance relating to it a hundred
times—She would have inquired, an' pleafe your honour, ten times as often about your honour's groin—
The pain, Trim, is equally excruciating———and
Compaffion has as much to do with the one as the
other——

——God blefs your honour! cried the corporal—
what has a woman's compaffion to do with a wound
upon the cap of a man's knee? had your honour's been
fhot into ten thoufand fplinters at the affair of Landen,
Mrs Wadman would have troubled her head as little
about

about it as Bridget; becaufe, added the corporal, low-
ering his voice, and fpeaking very diftinctly, as he affigned his reafon———

   " The knee is fuch a diftance from the main body—
whereas the groin, your honour knows, is upon the
very *curtain* of the *place*."

My uncle Toby gave a long whiftle—but in a note
which could fcarce be heard acrofs the table.

The corporal had advanced too far to retire———in
three words he told the reft———

My uncle Toby laid down his pipe as gently upon
the fender, as if it had been fpun from the unravellings
of a fpider's web—

—Let us go to my brother Shandy's, faid he.

CHAP. XXXII.

THERE will be juft time, whilft my uncle Toby
   and Trim are walking to my father's, to inform
you, that Mrs Wadman had, fome moons before this,
made a confident of my mother; and that Mis Bridget,
who had the burden of her own, as well as her miftrefs's fecret to carry, had got happily delivered of
both to Sufannah behind the garden wall.

As for my mother, fhe faw nothing at all in it, to
make the leaft buftle about—but Sufannah was fufficient, by herfelf, for all the ends and purpofes you
could poffibly have, in exporting a family fecret; for
fhe inftantly imparted it by figns to Jonathan—and
Jonathan by tokens to the cook, as fhe was bafting a
loin of mutton; the cook fold it with fome kitchen fat
to the poftilion for a groat, who truck'd it with the
dairy-maid for fomething of about the fame value—
and though whifper'd in the hay-loft, FAME caught
the notes with her brazen-trumpet, and founded them
upon the houfe top————In a word, not an old woman in the village or five miles round, who did not
underftand the difficulties of my uncle Toby's fiege,
and what were the fecret articles which had delayed
the furrender. ———

My father, whofe way was to force every event in
nature into an hypothefis, by which means never man
crucified

erucified Tʀᴜᴛʜ at the rate he did——had but juſt
heard of the report as my uncle Toby ſet out ; and
catching fire ſuddenly at the treſpaſs done his brother
by it, was demonſtrating to Yorick, notwithſtanding
my mother was ſitting by—not only, " That the devil
was in women, and that the whole of the affair was
luſt;" but that every evil and diſorder in the world,
of what kind or nature ſoever, from the firſt fall of
Adam, down to my uncle Toby's (incluſive) was owing one way or other to the ſame unruly appetite.

Yorick was juſt bringing my father's hypotheſis to
ſome temper, when my uncle Toby entering the room
with marks of infinite benevolence and forgiveneſs in
his looks, my father's eloquence rekindled againſt the
paſſion—and as he was not very nice in the choice of
his words when he was wroth—as ſoon as my uncle
Toby was ſeated by the fire, and had filled his pipe,
my father broke out in this manner.

C H A P. XXXIII.

—THAT proviſion ſhould be made for continu-
ing the race of ſo great, ſo exalted and god-
like a Being as man—1 am far from denying——but
philoſophy ſpeaks freely of every thing; and therefore
I ſtill think, and do maintain it to be a pity, that it
ſhould be done by means of a paſſion which bends down
the faculties, and turns all the wiſdom, contemplations,
and operations of the ſoul backwards—a paſſion, my
dear, continued my father, addreſſing himſelf to my
mother, which couples and equals wiſe men with fools,
and makes us come out of our caverns and hiding-
places more like ſatyrs and four-footed beaſts than
men.

I know it will be ſaid, continued my father, (availing
himſelf of the *Prolepſis*) that in itſelf, and ſimply taken
—like hunger or thirſt, or ſleep—'tis an affair neither
good or bad—or ſhameful or otherwiſe——Why then
did the delicacy of Diogenes and Plato ſo recalcitrate
againſt it? and wherefore, when we go about to make
and plant a man, do we put out the candle? and for
what reaſon is it, that all the parts thereof—the congre-
dients

dients—the preparations—the inſtruments, and whatever ſerves thereto, are ſo held as to be conveyed to a
cleanly mind by no language, tranſlation, or periphraſis
whatever ?

——The act of killing and deſtroying a man, continued my father, raiſing his voice—and turning to my
uncle Toby—you ſee is glorious—and the weapons by
which we do it are honourable—We march with them
upon our ſhoulders————We ſtrut with them by our
ſides—We gild them—We carve them—We in-lay
them—We enrich them—Nay, if it be but a *ſcoundrel*
cannon, we caſt an ornament upon the breech of it—

—My uncle Toby laid down his pipe to intercede
for a better epithet————and Yorick was riſing up to
batter the whole hypotheſis to pieces——

——When Obadiah broke into the middle of the
room with a complaint, which cried out for an imme-
diate hearing.

The caſe was this :

My father, whether by ancient cuſtom of the manor,
or as impropriator of the great tythes, was obliged to
keep a Bull for the ſervice of the Pariſh, and Obadiah
had led his cow upon a *pop-viſit* to him one day or
other the preceding ſummer—I ſay, one day or other
—becauſe, as chance would have it, it was the day on
which he was married to my father's houſe-maid—ſo
one was a reckoning to the other   Therefore, when
Obadiah's wife was brought to bed—Obadiah thanked
God——

—Now, ſaid Obadiah, I ſhall have a calf : ſo Obadiah went daily to viſit his cow.

She'll calve on Monday—or Tueſday—or Wedneſ-
day at the fartheſt——

The cow did not calve——No—ſhe'll not calve till
next week—the cow put it off terribly—till at the end
of the ſixth week, Obadiah's ſuſpicions (like a good
man's) fell upon the Bull.

Now the pariſh being very large, my father's Bull,
to ſpeak the truth of him, was no way equal to the de-
partment; he had, however, got himſelf, ſomehow or
other, thruſt into employment—and as he went thro'
the

the bufinefs with a grave face, my father had a high opinion of him.

—Moft of the townfmen, an' pleafe your worfhip, quoth Obadiah, believe that 'tis all the Bull's fault—

——But may not a cow be barren? replied my father, turning to Dr Slop.

It never happens, faid Dr Slop: but the man's wife may have come before her time naturally enough—— Pr'ythee has the child hair upon his head? added Dr Slop——

—It is hairy as I am; faid Obadiah.—Obadiah had not been fhaved for three weeks—Wheu u - - - u - - - - - - - cried my father; beginning the fentence with an exclamatory whiftle—and fo, brother Toby, this poor Bull of mine, who is as good a Bull as ever p—fs'd, and might have done for Europa herfelf in purer times—had he but two legs lefs, might have been driven into Doctors Commons and loft his character—which to a Town Bull, brother Toby, is the very fame thing as his life——

L—d! faid my mother, what is all this ftory about?——

A COCK and a BULL, faid Yorick—And one of the beft of its kind, I ever heard.

THE END.

9 NO64